"The church in the West is ⟨...⟩ when the need has never been ⟨...⟩ ⟨...⟩ ⟨...⟩ for the church to tell the world the good news in Jesus. Daniel Hames and Michael Reeves take us to the heart of the biblical motivation to share Christ: a proper vision of our great and glorious God. The more we are overflowing with the glorious love of God, the more we will overflow with words of the gospel to others. This book will show you how to overflow with gospel love."

Ed Stetzer, Executive Director, Wheaton College Billy Graham Center

"I could hardly put this book down—it made my heart sing. Hames and Reeves offer immensely joyful and faith-building encouragement to all who love and long to enjoy and participate in God's mission."

Gloria Furman, coeditor, *Joyfully Spreading the Word*; author, *Missional Motherhood*

"After decades of mission work, I've witnessed the various motivations driving missionary efforts, from the worst (a guilty conscience or vain ambition) to the good (a genuine concern for the lost). But Hames and Reeves call us to remember the best: that knowing and loving God deeply, fully, with a reckless abandon is our first and most essential priority for missions. They make it clear that when we truly know the nature of our loving, giving, gracious God, when we delight in him, we have the true fuel from God for missions. Don't let anyone you know go to the mission field without reading this book."

J. Mack Stiles, former Pastor, Erbil Baptist Church, Iraq

"The big idea of this book is both simple and life-transforming: 'It is precisely *because* God is outgoing and communicative that he is so good and delightful.' Thus, as this God's beloved people delight in him, they are propelled to speak about his goodness to others by communicating the good news. Yes, evangelism is a biblically commanded duty for all Christians. Yes, the Great Commission is a scripturally grounded purpose of the church. Yes, missions is a theologically supported enterprise for the benefit of the world. Ultimately, however, this endeavor is an overflow from knowing God. This book gets this truth right!"

Gregg R. Allison, Professor of Christian Theology, The Southern Baptist Theological Seminary; Secretary, Evangelical Theological Society; author, *Historical Theology*; *Sojourners and Strangers*; and *Embodied*

"Missiology tends to be long on pragmatics and short on theology. What a mistake! This book grounds our missiology in our theology, and provides a vision for how the truths of the Bible shape us and authentically motivate us toward the Great Commission."

Josh Moody, Senior Pastor, College Church, Wheaton, Illinois; President and Founder, God Centered Life Ministries

*WHAT FUELS THE
MISSION OF THE CHURCH?*

Union

A book series edited by Michael Reeves

Rejoice and Tremble: The Surprising Good News of the Fear of the Lord, Michael Reeves (2021)

What Does It Mean to Fear the Lord?, Michael Reeves (2021, concise version of *Rejoice and Tremble*)

Deeper: Real Change for Real Sinners, Dane C. Ortlund (2021)

How Does God Change Us?, Dane C. Ortlund (2021, concise version of *Deeper*)

The Loveliest Place: The Beauty and Glory of the Church, Dustin Benge (2022)

Why Should We Love the Local Church?, Dustin Benge (2022, concise version of *The Loveliest Place*)

God Shines Forth: How the Nature of God Shapes and Drives the Mission of the Church, Daniel Hames and Michael Reeves (2022)

What Fuels the Mission of the Church?, Daniel Hames and Michael Reeves (2022, concise version of *God Shines Forth*)

WHAT FUELS THE MISSION OF THE CHURCH?

DANIEL HAMES AND MICHAEL REEVES

CROSSWAY®

WHEATON, ILLINOIS

What Fuels the Mission of the Church?

Copyright © 2022 by Daniel Hames and Michael Reeves

Published by Crossway
        1300 Crescent Street
        Wheaton, Illinois 60187

Cover design: Jordan Singer

Cover image: Photo © Christie's Images / Bridgeman Images

First printing 2022

Printed in the United States of America

Trade paperback ISBN: 978-1-4335-7518-1
ePub ISBN: 978-1-4335-7521-1
PDF ISBN: 978-1-4335-7519-8
Mobipocket ISBN: 978-1-4335-7520-4

Library of Congress Cataloging-in-Publication Data

Names: Hames, Daniel, author. | Reeves, Michael (Michael Richard Ewert), author.
Title: What fuels the mission of the church? / Daniel Hames and Michael Reeves.
Other titles: God shines forth
Description: Wheaton, Illinois : Crossway, 2022. | Series: Union | Includes bibliographical
    references and index.
Identifiers: LCCN 2022005084 (print) | LCCN 2022005085 (ebook) | ISBN
    9781433575181 (trade paperback) | ISBN 9781433575198 (pdf) | ISBN 9781433575204
    (mobipocket) | ISBN 9781433575211 (epub)
Subjects: LCSH: Spirituality—Christianity. | Mission of the church. | Missions—Theory.
Classification: LCC BV4501.3 .H3535 2022b (print) | LCC BV4501.3 (ebook) | DDC
    248—dc23/eng/20220528
LC record available at https://lccn.loc.gov/2022005084
LC ebook record available at https://lccn.loc.gov/2022005085

Crossway is a publishing ministry of Good News Publishers.

VP   31   30   29   28   27   26   25   24   23   22
15   14   13   12   11   10   9   8   7   6   5   4   3   2   1

For Paul and Janey Hames
Psalm 113

Contents

Series Preface

OUR INNER CONVICTIONS AND VALUES shape our lives and our ministries. And at Union—the cooperative ministries of Union School of Theology, Union Publishing, Union Research, and Union Mission (visit www.theolo.gy)—we long to grow and support men and women who will delight in God, grow in Christ, serve the church, and bless the world. This Union series of books is an attempt to express and share those values.

They are values that flow from the beauty and grace of God. The living God is so glorious and kind, he cannot be known without being adored. Those who truly know him will love him, and without that heartfelt delight in God, we are nothing but hollow hypocrites. That adoration of God necessarily works itself out in a desire to grow in Christlikeness. It also fuels a love for Christ's precious bride, the church, and a desire humbly to serve—rather than use—her. And, lastly, loving God brings us to share his concerns, especially to see his life-giving glory fill the earth.

Each exploration of a subject in the Union series will appear in two versions: a full volume and a concise one. The concise treatments, such as this one, are like shorter guided tours: they stick to the main streets and move on fast. You may find, at the end of this little book, that you have questions or want to explore some more: in that case, the fuller volume will take you further up and further in.

My hope and prayer is that these books will bless you and your church as you develop a deeper delight in God that overflows in joyful integrity, humility, Christlikeness, love for the church, and a passion to make disciples of all nations.

Michael Reeves
SERIES EDITOR

Introduction

The Great Admission

LET'S GET IT OUT IN THE OPEN right at the beginning. Doesn't something about mission and evangelism just feel "off" to you? Every Christian knows we're meant to share the gospel and look for opportunities to witness to Christ, yet almost all of us find it a genuine struggle, if not a gloomy discouragement. The vital, final thing Jesus left his followers to do—the Great Commission!—seems to be the one thing about the Christian life that, frankly, doesn't feel so great. While we've heard the motivational sermons, sat in the "how to" seminars, and tried to crank ourselves up to initiating a deep conversation with friends or colleagues, we're often left feeling awkward and ashamed.

Complicating matters is that most of us *do* have a sincere desire that the people we love would come to know the Lord as we do. It's just that this longing doesn't seem to translate very easily or very often into actual evangelism. Any passion and boldness we may have in prayer apparently evaporates under the spotlight at the dinner table or on the coffee break. Our words dry up, our confidence deserts us, and we could wish we were almost anywhere else in the world.

If this all sounds familiar to you, you are not alone. So, what is going on? What is the mysterious cause of our complicated relationship with mission?

Perhaps insecurity keeps us from evangelism. We worry what other people might think of us if we start "Bible-thumping," so we keep quiet. Perhaps our problem is fear of failure. We don't feel well enough equipped or aren't confident enough in the power of the gospel, so we dare not risk rejection or (perhaps worse) indifference. These things may play a part in our predicament, but the diagnosis doesn't quite fit the symptoms. Personal insecurity or fear of failure seems to presuppose a burning passion in us to share the gospel that is simply being inhibited by some external barriers needing to be removed. A little training or a good pep talk could have us out on the streets in no time, fulfilling our hearts' desire to proclaim Christ every moment of every day!

But here is the great admission that many of us need to make: when it comes to the Great Commission, our *hearts* aren't really in it. Something far deeper than practical limitations is causing our mission fatigue.

Here's the Catch

If we are entirely honest, when we think about evangelism, we often feel something close to resentment. Many of us silently grumble that, in being recruited to evangelism, we're being put upon. We first came to know Jesus very happily, receiving his mercy and his invitation to new life, but then along came this unexpected and slightly puzzling additional step of having to be a witness to him in the world. Like a car shifting into the wrong gear, we came to a juddering halt. We'd been *offered* free grace and forgiveness, but now there's a *demand*? Christianity, we fear, was just too good to be true. Mission is the inevitable catch tacked on to the list of benefits we signed up for. It's the complicated, unwelcome add-on to salvation that God has included in the deal as the sweetener for himself.

But it seems that the Christian is left with no choice. In light of everything God has done for us, we owe him—and this is what he's stipulated. Having been drawn in by promises of easy yokes and light burdens, we have the sensation of being trapped in a contractual obligation. The thought of enjoying God forever had sounded warm and inviting, but the very word *evangelism* can send a chill down the spine. The worst of it is that all this ultimately reflects very badly on God, who begins not to look so good and attractive as we first thought. Like a PR agency representing a difficult client, we begin to wonder what we've got ourselves into. This reveals the real issue. The problem at the root of all our struggles with mission is almost certainly right at the beginning: with our view of God.

Getting God Right

If we believe that God is simply out to impose himself on the world and suck it dry of glory and praise, then we will never love and want to share him (even if we tell ourselves that God is entitled to do whatever he wants). If God seems to us a demanding taskmaster, we will never be his eager ambassadors in the world. If we feel ourselves conned into having to perform evangelism, we will never warm to the calling he has set before us. Unless we honestly find God to be beautiful and enjoyable, we'll have nothing worth saying to the people around us.

So this book is an invitation to start again at the beginning with your vision of God. Our aim is to set before your eyes God as he truly is: God who is so full of life and goodness that he loves to be known; not as a campaign to *impose* himself on us or on the world but to *give* himself and *share* his own life with the world. We want to show that the God of mission is no different from the God of the gospel. In fact, it is precisely *because* God is outgoing and communicative that he is so good and delightful. His natural fullness and superabundance mean that he does not need to *take* or *demand* from us but freely and kindly loves to *bless* us. His mission is not to wring out the world for every last drop but to *fill* it with his own divine joy and beauty. Seeing *this* glorious God will change everything for us.

Mission is no clunky add-on to your own delighting in God. Instead, it is the natural overflow and expression of the enjoyment you have of him so that, *like him*, you gladly go out to fill the world with the word of his goodness.

Our going out to the world with the gospel is not an endeavor that Christians have to hitch on to knowing God, bringing to the task a vigor and vim outsourced from elsewhere. Rather, the reality of God is itself at once all the motivation, the content, and the zest of our going. It is precisely because God, from his own glorious fullness, fills us with joy in him that we begin to bubble over with it to those around. The wellspring of healthy, happy mission is God himself.

1

The Glory of God

HAPPY MISSION PRESUPPOSES HAPPY CHRISTIANS.

There is a kind of mission that can be carried out by miserable Christians, and though it may be doctrinally correct and carefully organized, it will only reflect the emptiness in their own hearts. Christians who don't *enjoy* God can't and won't wholeheartedly commend him to others. If we fear that God's love for us is reluctant or that his approval rests on our performance, we won't feel any real affection for him, our service will be grudging, and the world will likely see through us.

At the heart of happy Christianity is knowing God rightly, which means beginning all our thinking with Jesus Christ.

Step into the Light

Jesus says, "All things have been handed over to me by my Father, and no one knows the Son except the Father, and no one knows the Father except the Son and anyone to whom the Son chooses to reveal him" (Matt. 11:27). The truth of God is naturally hidden from the world in the closed loop of relationship between the Father and the Son, and none of us can guess our way in. Only the Son, the one who knows the Father, can open this knowledge to us. Anyone can come to know the living God and find rest in him, but it is uniquely to *Jesus* they must come.

John calls Jesus "the true *light*, which gives light to everyone" (John 1:9). Here we meet a very common scriptural theme: that of the Son *enlightening* us. Paul does the same in 2 Corinthians 4 when he speaks of "the *light* of the gospel of the glory of Christ, who is the image of God" (v. 4). Indeed, he writes that "God, who said, 'Let light shine out of darkness,' has *shone in our hearts* to give the light of the knowledge of the glory of God *in the face of Jesus Christ*" (v. 6).

Time and again, Scripture is clear that sinful humanity languishes in unknowing darkness, but that the work of Jesus is to be the light in the dark rooms of our hearts and minds, showing us the Father.

Source and Beam

Since Jesus *is* himself God—the eternal Son of the Father—he is God *with* us. Not an expert lecturer or detailed commentator we may learn from, but God in person, reaching out to us to be known by us.

The writer to the Hebrews describes Jesus as the "exact imprint" or perfect representation of God to us, and also "the radiance of the glory of God" (1:3). To speak of Jesus as the "radiance" of God's glory is to say that Jesus is not a light directed at some *other* subject, like a flashlight pointed at your shoes in a tent at night. Radiance, like the sun and its beams, speaks of something—or someone—that, by nature, shines out and *gives* light. In other words, it is not that God is hiding in the dark and we must enlist Jesus to help us seek him out. Rather, God himself *is* the source of that light that comes to us in Christ. Put another way, the light that shines on us in Jesus *is* the light of the Father. The Father and the Son are one being, one God. The eternal life of God *is* the Father begetting his Son in the Holy Spirit. What we see in Jesus is not peripheral to the being of God. No, the Father, radiating his Son, shines like the sun in the sky and, by those beams, communicates himself to us.

In the radiance of Jesus, we not only are learning something *about* God but are *receiving God himself.*

Jesus, the Glory of God

Jesus *is* the glory of God: the very outshining radiance of his being.

Scripturally, glory has to do with the "weight" or "copious-ness" of something—its sheer, unmissable presence, especially in bright, shining splendor. For Jesus Christ to be the "radiance of the glory of God" is for him to be the weight or the substance of God impressed upon us, beaming on us, *given* to us.

When John went with Peter and James up the mountain and saw the Lord transfigured (Matt. 17:1–5), amid all the brightness and light, what is trumpeted most clearly is the Father's complete approval of his Son. Nothing and nobody else could more completely unveil, display, and thus please God the Father. In Jesus, we see the very being of God shining forth on us. He shows us a God who is fundamentally outgo-ing, outshining, and self-giving. He wants to be known by us, to be with us, even possessed by us, so that we will call him *our* God (Jer. 31:33).

Mission's Motor

If someone were to ask us, "What is God like?" the answer must be "Jesus Christ." And this is the beating heart of mission.

God's glory—his own naturally overspilling life, seen in his Son—is mission's *rationale* and its motor. In whatever sense mis-sion is about our going out into the world to make God known, it is only ever our being caught up in the already gushing tide of blessing that flows from the heart of the Father in the Son.

Those who bask in the sunshine of this loving and generous God are the happiest Christians and the happiest missionaries. Seeing in Jesus what our God is really like causes us to shine like him. We come to share his great heart's desire that his love, goodness, and righteousness would bless all the world.

But we haven't said all that must be said about the glory of God. We haven't yet said everything that must be said about Jesus. There is a strange but brighter brightness we still need to unveil: his death for us.

2

The Lamb on His Throne

CHRISTIANS SPEAK QUITE A BIT about God's glory, but we don't always do so in a thoroughly *Christian* way. We treat glory as though its meaning were self-evident and self-explanatory, allowing our natural, human idea of glory to lead the charge in our imaginations. In our fallen thinking, for God to be glorious is simply for him to be *great*.

But when we begin to see Jesus himself as the Glory of the Father and let him shape our idea of glory, we find that God is far better than we ever dared to believe, and his glory, beautifully different from our own. Nowhere is this more sharply detailed—and nowhere is the glory of God more tightly defined in Scripture—than on the cross of Jesus.

In the Throne Room

In the book of Revelation, the apostle John has a glimpse behind the curtain of the cosmos. As he looks into the great spiritual realities of the heavenly realm, he sees a throne (Rev. 4:3). The living God is seated there, and in his hand is a sealed scroll (Rev. 5:1). This scroll, we learn through the book, contains the meaning of history and the great arc of the purposes of God in it all, and nobody can open it and unlock its mysteries except "the Lion of the Tribe of Judah" (Rev. 5:5). Yet, as John watches, he sees not a roaring lion, but "a Lamb standing, as though it had been slain" (Rev. 5:6). The Lamb takes the scroll and opens the seals, and the company of heaven sings to him,

> Worthy are you to take the scroll
>   and to open its seals,
> for you were slain, and by your blood you ransomed
>   people for God
>   from every tribe and language and people and nation.
>   (Rev. 5:9)

Here is the most surprising and counterintuitive message. We would never have expected the God of glory and all his purposes to be revealed *this* way: in death. Yet *the Lamb who was slain* is specifically presented as the key to understanding it all.

Paul writes that the cross is the point at which God slices into our human ways of thinking—so thoroughly distorted and polluted by sin—to confront us and contradict us. Our natural assumption is that the crucifixion of the Son of God would be "folly" (1 Cor. 1:18), when in fact it is "the power of God and the wisdom of God" displayed (1 Cor. 1:24). If we want to know the true power and wisdom of God, then it is to the cross we must look.

Blood and Glory

So how are we to relate the glory of God to the cross? If Christ is the radiance of God's glory, is the crucifixion not the Glory of God himself being snuffed out? This is an important question, because many of us see the grace and mercy on display in Jesus's death for us but fear it was nothing more than an episode of atypical friendliness in God. Wonderfully, John's Gospel speaks of Jesus's death *as his glory*.

In John 2, Jesus attends the wedding in Cana where the wine runs out. When his mother, Mary, asks him to step in and help, he puzzlingly replies, "My hour has not yet come" (v. 4). Nevertheless, he turns water into wine, to the delight of the wedding guests, and John notes, "This, the first of his signs, Jesus did at Cana in Galilee, and manifested his glory" (v. 11). This sets up questions that hang over the rest of his Gospel. When will be the "hour" or moment to which Jesus is referring? What is the "glory" he is manifesting?

When Jesus enters the city of Jerusalem in John 12, everything falls into place at once. He says that, at long last, "the hour has come for the Son of Man to be glorified" (v. 23). Immediately he prays to his Father: "Now is my soul troubled. And what shall I say? 'Father, save me from this hour'? But for this purpose I have come to this hour. Father, glorify your name" (vv. 27–28). Then he speaks of being "lifted up from the earth" to "show by what kind of death he was going to die" (vv. 32–33).

The hour of Jesus's glorification is nothing other than the soul-troubling death that lies before him. The glory—the weight and substance of *who he is*—is to be set out for all to see on the cross. This was his purpose from the beginning, and not only his glorification but the Father's glorification *in him*. Jesus considers the "hour" in which he is hoisted up in shame and agony on the tree to be the moment of his glory and of his Father's great pleasure in him. Could it be that, in the horror of Golgotha, we see played out before us the *love and glory* of the Father and Son? That God shows us most deeply and wonderfully who he is in this sacrifice of himself?

The Roman soldiers cannot have known the truth they were preaching as they mockingly laid on him the purple robe and crown of thorns, fixing to his cross the sign "the King of the Jews." For here was the King of the universe bearing in himself all the curse (Gen. 3:18); the Lamb taking up his throne. Against all our fears, the cross was not a detour for God the Son. It was and is his glory. It is his glory that his soul should be troubled so that ours need not be (John 12:27; 14:1), that he himself should go down into the grave to bear the fruit of our eternal life (John 12:24), that he should be crucified between two thieves, "numbered with the transgressors" (Isa. 53:12), in the fate that should have been ours. As the eternal one empties himself into history and his love is poured out in blood, just as the festal wine has been, we can only stand amazed and say, with Thomas, "My Lord and my God!" (John 20:28).

Who Is Like the Lord Our God?

The cross is glory in that God shows himself there decisively. The cross is the glorification of *the* Glory (the Son!) of God. It stands as the defining moment in God's relationship to all creation—the pinnacle and epitome of all he desires to show us of himself.

Doing theology from the cross is like going through the looking glass with Alice into a totally different way of seeing everything. In fact, it is a death-and-resurrection experience for us, as "the LORD kills and brings to life" (1 Sam. 2:6). The air on the other side is different, and there is a freshness and beauty that we never sensed before. No matter how we might have thought of God before, at the cross, we learn that God truly *loves* us sinners and has done everything necessary to redeem us and bring us to himself.

The revelation of God at the cross torpedoes our expectations of him. Where we have imagined him to be distant and severe, the cross says, "God so loved the world, that he gave his only Son" (John 3:16). Where we have imagined him demanding a perfection we cannot offer, the cross says, "God shows his love for us in that while we were still sinners, Christ died for us" (Rom. 5:8). Where we have imagined ourselves dropping out of God's favor by our frequent disobedience, the cross says: "If anyone does sin, we have an advocate with the Father, Jesus Christ the righteous. He is the propitiation for our sins" (1 John 2:1–2). This way, the cross kindly puts us to death, contradicting us in every way, totally upending our human ways of thinking. All this is completely beautiful to us as we sing with the psalmist,

Who is like the LORD our God,
     who is seated on high,
who looks far down
     on the heavens and the earth? (Ps. 113:5–6)

3

Fullness

IS GOD REALLY LIKE JESUS?

If Jesus truly is the radiance of the Father, then all the goodness we see demonstrated and enacted in Christ's living, dying, and rising flows from God's own eternal life and being.

I Am Who I Am

In Exodus 3, Moses meets the Lord at the burning bush and asks him, "What is your name?" The Lord answers, "I AM WHO I AM. . . . Say this to the people of Israel: 'I AM has sent me to you'" (v. 14). God has answered Moses with a sentence. But then he says, "*The LORD*, the God of your fathers, the God of Abraham, the God of Isaac, and the God of Jacob, has sent me to you" (v. 15). These two parallel answers are related. The name "LORD" in our Bibles stands in for the personal name of God, which, in turn, comes from the word for "I am." When we speak of "the LORD," we are, in effect, calling God "the One Who Is," for he does not receive his name, identity, or existence from anyone or anything else: the life of God is self-contained and self-sustaining. He does not depend on anything to be who he is: he simply and eternally *is*. God does not rely on anything outside himself, and he does not evolve or improve. Having fullness of being, how could he? God's eternal life is unbeatably perfect as it is.

This is God—Father, Son, and Spirit—before, beyond, and above all created things. Yet the triune life is not a fortress, shut up against the world. No, the very life of God—all that he is in himself—overflows.

The Infinite Happiness of God

God the Father has eternally given to his Son. "For as the Father has life in himself," Jesus says, "so he has granted the Son also to have life in himself" (John 5:26). The eternal life of God *is* the Father begetting his Son in the Holy Spirit. The nature and quality of this eternal life is revealed to us when, on the night of his arrest, Jesus prays, "Father . . . you *loved* me before the foundation of the world" (John 17:24).

The Father's default way of being is to be filled with pleasure in fellowship with his Son in the Spirit. This love is ground zero of all the blessings that spill out on us in the creation of the world and in the gospel. God's being in eternal, self-sufficient life is no departure from the goodness of Jesus. It is the very fountainhead of his—and our—happiness. From the fellowship of Father, Son, and Spirit, superabundant goodness *spreads*.

Say No to Needy Gods

The glorious fullness of the living God revealed in Jesus sets him apart from all other gods. Throughout the Old Testament, the idols that tempt the Israelites are constantly described as "empty," and they hollow out those who worship them. They require the shedding of human blood (1 Kings 18:28) and the sacrifice of precious children (2 Kings 23:10); they cannot bring the rain (Jer. 14:22); and while they gladly take offerings, they cannot save in the times of trouble (Jer. 11:12).

In Acts 19:28, when Paul has preached the gospel in Ephesus, Demetrius the idol maker complains that the "great goddess" Artemis will be "counted as nothing" if Paul wins converts. This is quite an admission! Artemis is "nothing" without her temple and her worshipers, who could leave her at any moment.

All false gods *need* worship and service and sustenance. Not being self-existent or full in themselves, they demand, consume, and are never satisfied. Like hungry and irritable toddlers, they tend to throw tantrums and strike fear into their devotees. They are never satisfied and must always be on the take. Meanwhile, nothing about our God is withdrawn or protective, as though he were lacking or needy. He alone is eternally good, loving, and full of life. It is his very nature to abound, to give, and to radiate.

You Open Your Hand

God's fullness sets him apart not only from idols but also from us creatures. Humanity is, by nature, dependent and needy. Not only do we receive our life in the first place (unlike the Lord), but also we need to eat, drink, and sleep in order for that life to continue. God, who has life in himself, must *bestow* it on us, and God, who is eternal, must *preserve* us in that life.

Every time we hungrily sit down to a meal or collapse into bed, we are confronted with our own limits and finitude—our need to take something in before we can begin to give out again. It is no accident that we are this way.

You are created to desire and crave—and to have poured into you from outside—life and sustenance, whether physical or spiritual. The Lord has made us this way to show that he alone is the source of life and that we must go to him for it. Our very nature as human beings is to be contingent, always looking to our ever-giving God for life and everything.

The eyes of all look to you,
     and you give them food in due season.

You open your hand;

    you satisfy the desire of every living thing.

        (Ps. 145:15–16)

Full and Empty Living

For too many of us, our experience of the Christian life and of mission feels as though it is running on empty. Our view of God has slowly become distorted and skewed, so we do not set out filled with joy and satisfaction in him. In our efforts to serve a demanding god of our imaginations, our discipleship and evangelism feel eked out, because they are not fueled by an all-generous, giving God. If our God is not full, neither will we be.

But when we come to look at God in the light of Christ, we see that our God is an eternal spring of happiness and goodness, completely and irrepressibly *full*—full of glory, full of life, and full of blessing for the world. He is no black hole, eternally swallowing up glory, but an everlasting sun, *radiating* glory to the farthest reaches of our darkness. In Christ, God beams upon us, reveals his goodness, and shares himself with us. His happy fullness—and our derived enjoyment of him—is the heartbeat of mission, too.

4

Emptiness

IF GOD IS REALLY SO GOOD, surely mission must be the easiest work in the world. Simply hold out Jesus in his gospel, and people should come flocking.

Of course, that's not how it is. Quite the opposite. Bizarrely, the wonderful good news of free grace is a tough sell. People dislike not just the idea of God in general but the message of the gospel specifically. Human beings are fallen, and this is why we do not intuitively worship, trust, and love God. The radiance of God's glory shines not into neutrality but into *darkness*. The truth is that human beings, originally made in the image of God to love and enjoy him, reflecting his radiance in the world, have become *in*glorious through turning away from him.

Made for Glory

We were created to live in the presence and blessing of God. The first couple, Adam and Eve, were placed in the paradise of Eden, which God himself had planted for them, and where they were to enjoy fellowship with him. From the garden, they were to rule over the creation, multiplying to fill it (Gen. 1:28; 2:8).

Paul writes that Adam was a "type," or pattern, of Christ, "the one who was to come" (Rom. 5:14), because his purpose was to picture the one man who has always enjoyed the love of his Father (John 17:24), to whom every knee would one day bow (Phil. 2:10), and who would come to fill all things (Eph. 1:23). Here is the root of our sense of dignity, the reason we feel an itch for purpose and significance. We were created *for* glory and to *be* glorious, like our God.

Enslaved to Emptiness

Sin unraveled all this. More than simply disobeying a command and getting himself into trouble, Adam in his fall turned away from the Lord, the fountain of all life and love. The aftermath was devastating, for in denying God, Adam also defaced himself, enslaving himself and all his children to emptiness.

"Man is like a breath [literally, "emptiness"]," says David; "his days are like a passing shadow" (Ps. 144:4). It is now impossible for us to imagine life and humanity before the fall of Adam.

Like a laptop computer with the power cord unplugged, even the life we appear to hold within us is gradually ebbing away. Disconnected from the ever-full source of life and light and love, we are but waning shadows of all we were intended to be.

> All flesh is grass,
>> and all its beauty is like the flower of the field.
> The grass withers, the flower fades
>> when the breath of the LORD blows on it;
>> surely the people are grass.
> The grass withers, the flower fades
>> but the word of our God will stand forever.
>> (Isa. 40:6–8)

The Image Defaced

Our fallen emptiness means we cannot be radiant as we were meant to be. When, in the fall, Adam ceased to look to God and looked instead to himself (even to his own body in its nakedness and vulnerability, Gen. 3:7), the crucial bond between the divine image and the image bearer was broken. The image of God in humanity was defaced, and the glory dimmed.

Adam's loss of glory became the family trait. As well as being infected with his guilt and his death, each of bears his likeness in behavior, "for all have sinned and fall short of the glory of

God" (Rom. 3:23). It would be wrong to say that fallen people no longer bear the image of God at all: sin has not entirely destroyed all that God created. Nevertheless, the image is spoiled and marred such that we do not shine out with the glory of God.

With our eyes off God in his glory and forever flitting about in the darkest corners, we are gradually formed into the image of creatures that deprive us of the life we miss and cannot satisfy us or restore us to our proper place. However frustrated and unfulfilled we find ourselves, we nevertheless settle into unhappy cycles of worshiping nothingness, with nothing to gain and nothing to give out.

This lies behind what can feel like the most perplexing response we encounter in evangelism: apathy. This reaction may frustrate the evangelist, but it should provoke our compassion. It is the fruit of a heart that is simultaneously deeply unsatisfied and without hope of satisfaction. The emptiness of sin is so profound that it leaves us hardened and stagnant.

Mirror, Mirror, on the Wall . . .

Given all we have seen, it is no wonder that our culture is overrun with issues surrounding identity. Since the garden, we do not participate in the fullness of God's life, his image in us has been vandalized, and we are consumed with self-love. Sinners do not know who, why, or what they are. Many people want to improve themselves but simply do not know what "mended" or whole people would look like. Sensing our brokenness, we make wild stabs at solutions: political activism, radical moral codes, mindfulness, self-improvement, dieting fads, and so on.

Feeling our emptiness, we crave the praise and attention of other people, making ourselves hostage to their opinions. We may find ourselves emotionally leaning on others too heavily, forcing friendships or romantic relationships to carry a weight of expectation they are unable to bear. Anxiety, stress, depression, and loneliness soon follow.

The emptiness and darkness of this present age form the context and backdrop of the mission of the church (Titus 2:12). They mark the condition of the people around us who must hear the gospel of the glory of God if they are to be set free. The church alone can show the world where real fullness, happiness, and life are to be found.

5

Born in Zion

WHAT WAS GOD TO DO WITH HUMANITY, lost in this darkness and futility? God *reached out*. Christ came to *remake* us after his image.

This is where our mission began. For this renewal of human beings is not only the birth of *Christians* but the birth of *missionaries*, as we who once were darkness become "light in the Lord" (Eph. 5:8).

When the psalmist applauds the glory of Zion in Psalm 87, he includes a surprising list of inhabitants: Rahab, Babylon, Philistia, Tyre, and Cush (v. 4). These are Gentile outsiders being counted as residents of Zion, included with Israel, fully belonging as though they were born in the city of God. The psalmist says of each, "This one was born there" in Zion (v. 4). By God's grace, out of Rahab and Babylon, from darkness and nothingness, new life is found and a new identity is established. Those who once were far off have been brought near to share in the call to proclaim the gospel in the world (Eph. 2:11–13).

The Image Restored

In Adam, humanity had slipped far from its noble purpose in creation, leaking life, falling short of God's glory, and turning in on itself in idolatry and selfishness. But Jesus Christ came into the world to turn us around.

Every moment of Jesus's life on earth was a display of humanity as it was always supposed to be. For the first time, a human being lived in the fullness of God's intentions for us. He perfectly loved, trusted, and obeyed his Father (John 14:31) and poured out his heart to him in prayer (Luke 6:12), even though he faced all the same temptation, weakness, and suffering we do (Heb. 2:18; 4:15). He was morally faultless himself but never lacked compassion for even the most notorious sinners (Mark 2:15–17). He exercised rule over the creation, stilling wind and waves (Matt. 8:27) and driving out the corruption of demons and diseases (Matt. 12:22–24). He amazed his disciples with words of truth that could only be God's own self-expression (Mark 10:24). He went silently to his death, giving himself in love for those who hated him (Mark 15:5). Full of life, gloriously good, and overflowing with kindness, Jesus was everything a human being is *meant* to be—the definitive likeness of God, revealed in the original image himself. Here, at last, was a real man.

The Great Exchange

Christ came not merely to set us an example to follow but also to take hold of humanity, binding himself to us and us to himself. He came to take the old humanity to the cross with him and put it to death, raising us with him in his resurrection. "Father," he prayed shortly before his crucifixion, "I desire that they also, whom you have given me, *may be with me where I am*" (John 17:24). Salvation is an exchange. He came into the wreckage of humanity, taking all our sin and death to himself on the cross, and he raised us to the fellowship with the Father that he himself eternally had.

Now, Christ's perfect life and righteousness are credited to us (2 Cor. 5:21), his resurrection is the guarantee of our own to come (Rom. 6:5), and we receive a whole catalog of spiritual blessings in and through him (Eph. 1:3–14).

You Have Been Filled in Him

On the other side of the cross, this redeemed human life is the "new self, which is being renewed in knowledge after the image of its creator" (Col. 3:10). The same Spirit who filled, led, and empowered Jesus (Matt. 12:28; Luke 4:1) now dwells in us (Eph. 2:22).

When the Colossian church was facing pressure to turn aside from Jesus to various extraneous spiritual practices, Paul wrote to reassure them of the complete sufficiency of Jesus and the life they already had in him:

> See to it that no one takes you captive by philosophy and empty deceit, according to human tradition, according to the elemental spirits of the world, and not according to Christ. *For in him the whole fullness of deity dwells bodily, and you have been filled in him.* (Col. 2:8—10)

With Jesus, we who naturally have nothing are given everything. Empty, hollow sinners are enriched, ennobled, and *filled* as we are united with the one who has in himself the fullness of God.

"Hearts Unfold like Flowers before Thee"

When we come to the cross of Christ and are filled by him, the first change we experience is in our relationship with God. We find ourselves increasingly warming with his love, unclenching our fists, and coming freely to adore and enjoy him. Unconsciously forgetting ourselves, we can sing,

Joyful, joyful, we adore Thee,
God of glory, Lord of love;
Hearts unfold like flowers before Thee,
opening to the sun above.[1]

Finding this treasure outside ourselves, we become refreshingly un-self-obsessed. Once, we cringed and retreated before the light, but now we are blossoming flowers, soaking up the sunshine. In humble, happy Christians, the glory of God is echoed back to him in gratitude. Now, turned inside out by the gospel of Jesus, we look out from ourselves toward God in worship. But there is a second opening up we experience too. We radiate outward into the world.

A Glorious Image

When empty ones are filled by the God of fullness, we become bright and glorious like him, for "we all, with unveiled face, beholding the glory of the Lord, are being transformed into the *same image* from *one degree of glory to another*" (2 Cor. 3:18). Christians take on Jesus's radiance.

Here is the birth of our mission, for the Christian's new birth is a birth into a life in the image of the God who is always on mission. Now born in Zion, we belong to the Lord and manifest his life in our own lives. Because this life is *his* gift—the

47

gift of the ever-outgoing, generous God—it is a *godly* life that delights to multiply, spread out, and increase. So believers become shining lights in the world, as he is *the* light of the world (Matt. 5:16; John 8:12), shining with his own light as we hold him out to "a crooked and twisted generation" (Phil. 2:14–16).

Cross-Shaped Living

Just as the cross reveals God to be full and glorious in love, humility, and blessing, so it creates Christians who are the same way. Happiness, beauty, and humility flow from the lives of those who are restored in *the* image of God. This transformation from our empty, fallen life to the glorious, truly human (Christlike!) life is at the heart of healthy mission. The cross makes mean souls into lavish souls.

The glory of the Christian is always Jesus Christ and him crucified. "Far be it from me to boast except in the cross of our Lord Jesus Christ," says Paul (Gal. 6:14). Knowing that we are empty ones, now full of him, we always place Jesus himself at the foreground rather than ourselves. It is Jesus we have to offer to the world.

6

Arise, Shine!

IF CHRISTIANS ARE RENEWED in the image of God, "born in Zion," and shining with the glory of the Lord, why does mission continue to be such a challenge for us?

Too often, we find ourselves fragile and timid in mission, propelled by a mixed bag of motivations and emotions. We may be totally committed to mission as an activity of the church but feel low on energy and enthusiasm. We know that despite everything being right in theory, something is still missing, and we are simply not sparkling with the beauty and goodness of Jesus. While we know God to be full, our mission feels empty. What is going on?

How to Be a Bad Missionary

Jesus reproved the religious leaders of his day for a distortion of mission that was not the fruit of happy hearts but the toil of spiritual captives.

> But woe to you, scribes and Pharisees, hypocrites! For you
> shut the kingdom of heaven in people's faces. For you neither
> enter yourselves nor allow those who would enter to go in.
> Woe to you, scribes and Pharisees, hypocrites! For you travel
> across sea and land to make a single proselyte, and when he
> becomes a proselyte, you make him twice as much a child
> of hell as yourselves. (Matt. 23:13–15)

The scribes and Pharisees belonged not to the kingdom of heaven but to hell, and they willingly went great distances for their "mission." Notice that Jesus referred to their fruit not as "converts" but as "proselytes." Self-justifying, empire-building evangelists may see many proselytes won by force of personality or impressive communication, but hypocrites can only give birth to hypocrites.

This is the very definition of "empty" mission—and it begins with a tragically thin view of God. Driven by the glory of people rather than of God (John 5:44), the Pharisees were insecure and petty (Matt. 12:2), willing to climb over others for attention, praying ostentatiously in public places, and comparing themselves with one another (Matt. 6:5; Luke 18:11). Pharisees cannot truly love God or other people, because they have not first enjoyed the love of God for themselves. When disciples of an empty, demanding god do mission, they will tend to be results-driven bullies. Even an evangelist who *preaches* a gospel of grace but is really justifying himself betrays the fact that God seems to him neither near nor kind—not truly gracious or glorious.

Sticks and Carrots

When Christians are not filled to overflowing with the glorious goodness of God, church leaders will have to find other motivations to drive them. Frequently, we will turn for help to the sinister twins: duty and debt.

It is not uncommon to hear conference speakers or youth leaders in drill sergeant mode, firing up their listeners with what amounts to little more than a guilt trip. The Christian duty is to "go into all the world," we are told, and only lazy, selfish believers have not already promised the Lord they will go anywhere, anytime if he calls. Since Jesus has done so much for you, how could you refuse him? Christians *can* be cajoled into evangelism like a herd of animals, but this is not a foundation for healthy and effective mission. Duty and debt are cruel motivations for mission. Those who try to draw on them will end up unconvinced salespeople who peddle a product they do not finally believe in or enjoy for themselves.

Deeper still, at the root of these motivations is an undelightful god, who keeps a record of our debts and accepts us in proportion to our performance. Unless Christians are carried into mission by genuine enjoyment of the Lord, their mission will not embody the glory of the living God.

There are also rewards we might set before Christians to engage them in mission. The carrot is mightier than the stick. We might dwell on the capacity of evangelism to deepen our own growth and sanctification. But, in the long run, even "carrots" do not work as ultimate motivations for mission. They are, by nature, *additions* to what believers already have in knowing God and cannot be the primary way the church fuels its mission. Happy mission is rooted not in our response to God but in *his own nature*. The truest and highest motivation for mission is God himself.

Cutting Out Christ

If we are not captured specifically by the glory of God in Christ, then it will be no surprise when our message quickly has little to do with him. If it is not *him* we are enjoying, it will not be *him* we convey to others. Even unwittingly, we may become ministers of another gospel (Gal. 1:7). It may not be the out-and-out false gospels of, for example, prosperity or "health and wealth," but something more subtle. Our tendency will be toward abstraction from God, focusing on things that, almost without our notice, are not quite Jesus Christ and him crucified. We may find ourselves emphasizing themes of the gospel like "grace" or "heaven" but not explicitly holding out *Christ* as the gift and as the treasure of heaven. We may offer the world the hope of transformed lives, healed hurts, and renewed communities, but make Jesus the *means* to these things rather than the center of them all. These things are blessings of the gospel, but if they are elevated to become its center and our focus, they will become nothing more than substitute gods.

God's mission is revealed in the sending of his Son, and the church is sent with the mission of heralding that same Son. Because of this, the proclamation of the gospel, the heralding of Christ, is the nonnegotiable of mission. Evangelism has *content* to it, and the content is Jesus Christ himself. In other words, our offering to the world is not ourselves but the Lord.

The God We Know Is the God We Show

If God seems to us to be empty and needy, we will serve him with empty hearts, finally taking what we need from the world rather than freely blessing it. What we truly worship and cherish will, for good or ill, be revealed in our mission. The God we know—or think we know—is the God we will show to the world.

Real, fruitful, healthy mission must begin with delight in God, for we become like the one we worship. His happiness makes us happy; his kindness makes us kind; his glory fills us. Then, made beautiful like our Lord, with compassion and verve we will carry the blessing of Jesus to the ends of the earth.

When Isaiah called the people of Israel to "arise, shine," it was because "your light has come, and *the glory of the LORD has risen upon you*" (60:1). This was no frustrated outburst, pushing them to "get up and jolly well get on with it," but a promise that, amid the darkness covering the world, "his glory will be seen upon you" (60:2). The Lord himself was to be with them, enlightening (60:3), enriching (60:5), and beautifying (60:9) them. As God shines upon his beloved redeemed people (60:16), so he will shine *out from* us.

7

Those Who Look to Him Are Radiant

THE FOUNDATION OF ALL OUR MISSION is our knowledge and enjoyment of God.

Yes, I may be born again, but I may not yet be a good missionary. I may have the right intellectual conviction about God's goodness but be unmoved by him. I may know just what to say and how to say it in my gospel presentation, honoring the Lord with my lips while remaining far from him in my heart (Isa. 29:13).

Our delight in God is the main fuel for mission.

A Good Theologian Is a Good Missionary

John Calvin knew well the vital union between knowing God and mission. Sending missionaries all over the world from

Geneva, he first gave them a solid theological foundation. "He believed that a good missionary had to be a good theologian first."[1] Indeed, a good theologian is a good missionary, *and* a good missionary is a good theologian. Those people who know God most deeply and satisfyingly will be the best at winning hearts into the kingdom; and those most thrilled at the prospect of taking the gospel out into the world are those most captured by the beauty and goodness of the God of the gospel.

This is nothing more than the teaching of Jesus in John 15, who calls his disciples to abide in him, "the true vine," if they would bear fruit (vv. 1–4). The only fruitful branches on the vine are those which abide in him, or specifically abide *in his love* (v. 9). Fruitful mission is certainly an activity: it requires going out and speaking up, and yet it can only be as the *fruit* of branches that have first learned to abide. Our happiness in Jesus's love is his priority for us, even above our sense of being useful to him; in fact, our fruitfulness depends on it.

The Glorious Ones

The Lord says:

> You are the light of the world. A city set on a hill cannot be hidden. Nor do people light a lamp and put it under a basket, but on a stand, and it gives light to all in the house. In the

same way, *let your light shine before others*, so that they may see your good works and give glory to your Father who is in heaven. (Matt. 5:14–16)

When Christians enjoy union and communion with the Lord, they are transformed into his likeness (2 Cor. 3:18). Where the Lord is present with his people, his very own light and life shine out.

Out of Zion, the perfection of beauty,
   God shines forth. (Ps. 50:2)

The light and glory of the church are no secondary light and glory but Christ himself.

When I Am Weak

Mission fueled by the fullness of God is able to deal with the weakness of its missionaries. Wounded soldiers, struggling saints, and stumbling preachers are not dismissed from the Lord's army, because they are not expected to be full in and of themselves. In our suffering, our battle with sin, and our lack of experience or boldness or eloquence, we are nonetheless invited to delight ourselves in the Lord and find fullness in him. Paul's experience with weakness led him to know Christ's power in him so deeply that he was content not to feign personal strength but to renounce it: "For when I am weak, then I am strong" (2 Cor. 12:10).

Even in our sin—our frequent denial of the Lord and of our new life in him—we are not finally empty but know the fullness of God. His mercies never come to an end, and his compassion does not fail (Lam. 3:22). The same Son of God who gave himself for us on the cross is, even now, a sympathetic high priest who continues to intercede for us as we struggle with temptation (Heb. 2:14; 4:15; 7:25).

Blood and Glory

This matchless love and grace to such empty ones is a fullness that takes us beyond ourselves. Adopted by a perfect Father, united to his glorious Son, and indwelt by the Comforter, Christians are able to take to the spiritual battlefield of mission with happy, humble selflessness.

Suffering in Jesus's service is something we are frequently told to expect. Paul writes, "It has been granted to you that for the sake of Christ you should not only believe in him but also suffer for his sake" (Phil. 1:29), and this is, in fact, a participation in Christ's own sufferings, which are a gateway to resurrection life (Phil. 3:10–11). Peter says that "if you are insulted for the name of Christ, you are *blessed, because the Spirit of glory and of God rests upon you*" (1 Pet. 4:14). On the cross, our captain has gone before us into the fight and has already conquered Satan, sin, and death. He has shed his blood and shown his glory. He has shown us a love that cannot be quenched, even by death (Song 8:6). We cannot lose!

Outside the Camp

In the law, the camp of Israel and her cities were to be kept ceremonially clean, and all that was defiled had to be ejected. Outside the camp was the only fit place for throwing out ashes and waste (Lev. 4:21); it was the colony of those afflicted with infectious diseases (Lev. 13:46) and the venue for the execution of blasphemers (Lev. 24:14). Yet Jesus went out from the center to prostitutes and tax collectors, lepers and Gentiles. Without being infected or compromised, he embraced them, welcomed them, and saved them. In fact, he himself "suffered outside the [city] gate" on the cross to make his people holy (Heb. 13:12). Because he is so full of purity and holiness, he was not diminished by touching death and disease, but his life blazed out, cleansing and healing, delivering, and making whole. He drove out not just unclean spirits but death itself.

Our own mission now is to "*go to him outside the camp* and bear the reproach he endured" (Heb. 13:13). Made alive, filled, and sanctified in Christ, we do not hide within the "camp" of the church but reach out. This outward stretching of the church, matching that of her Lord, is the extension of his kingdom and blessing into the world, his light shining, and his goodness spreading. Christ's church always moves into the world with a holiness that can bless, purify, and give life.

A Band of Brothers

Finally, this outward, selfless posture of the church in mission extends to those we find alongside us in the ranks. In a people filled with Jesus's all-embracing glory, there can be no room for tribalism, competition, and hidden agendas.

If I am delightedly filled by Christ, then I will happily march out shoulder to shoulder with brothers and sisters. If I believe that I am brilliant but you are weak, I will trek out alone without any care for you. But if I know my own wretched sinfulness and emptiness, I will be honored to go *together* with you. I will see Christ in you and feel amazed that I can count you a fellow laborer in the gospel (Phil. 2:25). Then, with honesty, humility, trust, and mutual encouragement, we will go out in mission as a happy fellowship.

Deep Down Delighting

Healthy, robust mission is never an accessory to knowing God. It is not an activist project that must be *added* to our enjoyment of him in salvation. Mission that is to be full and not empty flows only from the satisfaction we experience in Jesus Christ.

The fullness of God given to us in salvation sends us out in mission, but even as we go, we are drawn *toward* fullness too. Our present delight in God magnetically leads us toward the day when we will know his love not in part but in whole. The victories we see in mission as his kingdom advances anticipate the day the whole earth will see his glory.

8

We Will See Him as He Is

THE CULMINATION OF MISSION IS GLORY.
Habakkuk prophesied that

the earth will be filled
with the knowledge of the glory of the LORD
as the waters cover the sea. (2:14)

But what will this glory be like? Often when we try to imagine our life in eternity, we soon begin to ponder nervous, slightly guilty questions: Will I recognize my friends and family? Will my dog be there? Will I actually *enjoy* it? Underneath our fears is the suspicion that when God finally and fully reveals his glory—the weight and substance of his being and nature— it will turn out to be something *other* than the grace, goodness, and kindness displayed in the gospel. The self-giving glory of the cross will have been simply a means to another end: perhaps God's retirement to a life of isolated majesty, with troublesome humanity out of his hair.

Wonderfully, we could not be more wrong about God's plans.

The Revelation of Jesus Christ

The last book of the Bible is specifically about "the revelation of Jesus Christ" (Rev. 1:1) because it is *his* glory that will be fully unveiled on the last day. All the promises of God—including those about our future—find their "Yes" *in Jesus* (2 Cor. 1:20). In the gospel's promised future, we will eternally enjoy the very glory that fuels our lives and mission today. When Jesus returns, the spark of our *present* enjoyment of God and his gospel will be fanned into flame as all creation is saturated with the glory of our own dear Lord Jesus, the radiance of the Father.

The glory that we long for and hold out to the world is the very same outshining glory that propels our mission now.

God's Last Great End

This glorious end to the story is both the goal and the motivation of mission because it has *always* been God's design and intention for his creation. From the very beginning to the very end, God's purpose in all things is the demonstration of his glory. But the God who has been so selflessly kind to us throughout history is not planning to exit stage left with a selfish flourish of megalomania.

No, God has determined that his own outshining brings about *our* delight and joy in the end. He is *already* eternally happy in fellowship with his Son, and *that* is what will overflow to us and all creation in the end. God will make us eternally happy out of the sheer abundance of his own happiness.

Gracious Glory

Jesus's description of our "eternal life" in John 17:3 is specifically about enjoying fellowship with God: "that they know you, the only true God, and Jesus Christ whom you have sent." The life and glory that will one day fill the earth springs from the fountain of the everlasting love and delight of the Father, Son, and Spirit.

In this glory, we who are naturally far from God and tragically self-absorbed will be made eternally joyful and content, enfolded into indestructible fellowship with God. We who are in Christ will be drawn in to know and enjoy him further and more deeply than ever before, knowing in full what we now know only in part, seeing with crisp clarity what we now see only dimly of his beauty (1 Cor. 13:12). For God himself will come to *dwell with us* (Rev. 21:3). The one who once came as a "friend of tax collectors and sinners" (Luke 7:34) and loved them to death will prove himself devoted to us for endless ages.

On the last day, just as at Calvary, God who is full of life, light, and love will *pour himself out* for those who are naturally empty, gloomy, and unlovely. Flowing to us from the cross, his is an entirely *gracious* glory.

All Things New

The personal presence of the Lord will mean that all that has saddened and hurt us will be blasted away. The Lamb on heaven's throne will declare, "Behold, I am making all things new" (Rev. 21:5). God himself "will wipe away every tear from their eyes, and death shall be no more, neither shall there be mourning, nor crying, nor pain anymore, for the former things have passed away" (Rev. 21:4). He will finally drive out Satan and all evil from the world (Rev. 20:10). Death, the final enemy, will be destroyed, and all will be perfect, everlasting life (1 Cor. 15:26). You will have cried your last tear, grappled with guilt's last assault, suffered your last bereavement. For when the glory of the Lord fills the earth, we will live in a world with no more threat of danger, disease, and death.

What a hope to share with the world! In the drying of our tears, we see a God so filled with compassion that he personally stoops to comfort his people. In the last defeat of Satan, we see a God so beautifully pure that he will tolerate nothing that would harm his children. In the end of death, we see a God so generously full that he loves to give his life without measure such that death is blotted out forever. The hope of his coming is comfort for the weeping, the oppressed, and the dying today. *As we hold out the hope of the gospel in our broken world now, it is the full revelation of the loving God of the gospel that we anticipate.*

A World of Love

The defining characteristic of our future fellowship with God is his love for us. For God *is* love (1 John 4:8) and "love never ends" (1 Cor. 13:8).

In the life to come, we will love God more truly because we will finally have an unclouded appreciation of his love for us. Our love for others will also be transformed. In the light of God's love in heaven, nothing and nobody will be unlovely.

Can you imagine a life where you *know*, without any creeping anxiety, that you are perfectly and totally loved by God? Where you love him in return without any whisper of shame or inadequacy? A life where you are entirely secure in the love of those around you and are able to love them all without feeling exposed or vulnerable? Where you love people with such a generous freedom that you yourself only become more open and lovely?

This is life in the glory of God and the light of the Lamb who was slain. The grace we have found at the foot of the cross we will discover again and again in wave after infinite wave: the free giving of the superabundant one to those who are in themselves empty, needy, and longing.

Children of the Light

The promise of this life before us sustains us now in our ministry and mission. And it is precisely this hope that we hold out to the world.

Our mission carries the same glory as our hope. In 1 Thessalonians 5, Paul calls Christians "children of light," who do not belong to the darkness of this present and passing age (vv. 4–6). Because believers are filled with the life of Christ by the Spirit, we are lights in "this present darkness" (Eph. 6:12), beacons of divine glory in a sea of emptiness. In a sense, Christians are children of the future, living in the world with their sights set beyond it, knowing what is coming soon.

The church's mission is shaped and driven by the very nature of our God. All that we know of him, however limited by our present ignorance and sin, fills us with joy. Yet our hope of knowing him fully in the age to come can only increase our delight and anticipation, propelling us out into the world in overwhelmed gladness.

Happily Ever After

There is a reason that all the best stories end with a bride and groom living happily ever after: it is the one true story in the universe. At the end, Jesus Christ will fulfill his vows to his church.

The final mention of the Lamb in the book of Revelation comes in chapter 21 when he is married to his blood-bought bride. She is "the holy city Jerusalem coming down out of heaven from God, *having the glory of God*, its radiance like a most rare jewel" (vv. 10–11). This had been his heart's desire from the beginning (Song 2:10; Hos. 2:20). Yes, the culmination of history is the glory of God. Not glory taken but glory *given*. The whole creation suffused with his light, his creatures filled and made happy in his goodness, his bride drenched eternally in his love. We, the redeemed, can only sing,

> Worthy is the Lamb who was slain,
> to receive power and wealth and wisdom and might
> and honor and glory and blessing! (Rev. 5:12)

Notes

Chapter 5: Born in Zion

1. Henry Van Dyke, "Joyful, Joyful, We Adore Thee" (1907), https://hymnary.org.

Chapter 7: Those Who Look to Him Are Radiant

1. Frank A. James III, "Calvin the Evangelist," *Reformed Quarterly* 19, no. 2 (2001): 8.

Scripture Index

Union

We fuel reformation in churches and lives.

Union Publishing invests in the next generation of leaders with theology that gives them a taste for a deeper knowledge of God. From books to our free online content, we are committed to producing excellent resources that will refresh, transform, and grow believers and their churches.

We want people everywhere to know, love, and enjoy God, glorifying him in everything they do. For this reason, we've collected hundreds of free articles, podcasts, book chapters, and video content for our free online collection. We also produce a fresh stream of written, audio, and video resources to help you to be more fully alive in the truth, goodness, and beauty of Jesus.

If you are hungry for reformational resources that will help you delight in God and grow in Christ, we'd love for you to visit us at unionpublishing.org.

unionpublishing.org

Union Series

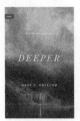

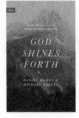

Full & Concise Editions

Rejoice and Tremble | *What Does It Mean to Fear the Lord?*

Deeper | *How Does God Change Us?*

The Loveliest Place | *Why Should We Love the Local Church?*

God Shines Forth | *What Fuels the Mission of the Church?*

The Union series invites readers to experience deeper enjoyment of God through four interconnected values: delighting in God, growing in Christ, serving the church, and blessing the world.

For more information, visit **crossway.org**.